Freaky Plant Facts

Extreme Greens

by Ellen Lawrence

Consultants:

Suzy Gazlay, MA
Recipient, Presidential Award for Excellence in Science Teaching

Dr. Robin Wall Kimmerer
Professor of Environmental and Forest Biology
SUNY College of Environmental Science and Forestry, Syracuse, New York

Kimberly Brenneman, PhD
National Institute for Early Education Research, Rutgers University
New Brunswick, New Jersey

BEARPORT
PUBLISHING

New York, New York

Credits

Cover © Kazuhiro Nogi/Getty Images; 3L, © Frank Walker/Alamy; 3R, © Wikipedia Creative Commons; 4–5, © Graham Barclay/Getty Images; 6L, © fotototo/Shutterstock; 6R, © Christian Musat/Shutterstock; 7, © age fotostock/Superstock; 9, © Vadim Petrakov/Shutterstock; 10, © Masalski Maksim/Shutterstock; 10–11, © S & D & K Maslowski/FLPA; 12TR, © eye35 stock/Alamy; 12B, © Imagebroker/FLPA; 13, © Vitaly Korolev; 14, © Kobe Kachoen/Wikipedia Creative Commons; 15, © Kazuhiro Nogi/Getty Images; 16, © Christian Fischer/Wikipedia Creative Commons; 16–17, © Sylvie Bouchard/Shutterstock; 18, © Wikipedia Creative Commons; 18–19, © age fotostock/Superstock; 20–21, © Martin B. Withers/FLPA; 22BL, © vnlit/Shutterstock; 22BR, © Nejron Photo/Shutterstock; 22 inset L, © Godunova Tatiana/Shutterstock; 22 inset R, © caimacanul/Shutterstock; 23TL, © David Lee/Shutterstock; 23TC, © Photobac/Shutterstock; 23TR, © Rob Marmion/Shutterstock; 23BL, © Michael Peuckert/FLPA and © Le Do/Shutterstock; 23BC, © Shell114/Shutterstock; 23BR, © Valery121283/Shutterstock.

Publisher: Kenn Goin
Editorial Director: Adam Siegel
Creative Director: Spencer Brinker
Design: Elaine Wilkinson
Photo Researcher: Ruby Tuesday Books Ltd

Library of Congress Cataloging-in-Publication Data

Lawrence, Ellen, 1967–
 Freaky plant facts : extreme greens / by Ellen Lawrence.
     p. cm. — (Plant-ology series)
 Includes bibliographical references and index.
 ISBN 978-1-61772-591-3 (library binding) — ISBN 1-61772-591-9 (library binding)
 1. Plants—Miscellanea—Juvenile literature. I. Title.
 QK49.L39 2013
 581—dc23
                              2012018625

For more information, write to Bearport Publishing Company, Inc., 45 West 21st Street, Suite 3B, New York, New York 10010. Printed in the United States of America.

10 9 8 7 6

Contents

What Is That Terrible Smell?

Crowds of people have gathered to see one of the biggest flowers on Earth.

The flower looks beautiful, but what is that awful stink?

Is it rotten meat or animal poop?

No! The smell is coming from the freaky flower.

The titan arum is one of the biggest flowers on Earth—and one of the smelliest!

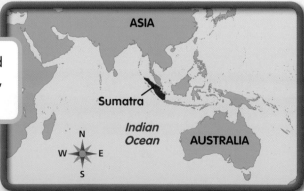

The titan arum grows wild in rain forests on Sumatra, an island in Asia.

ASIA

Sumatra

Indian Ocean

AUSTRALIA

N
W · E
S

titan arum flower

A titan arum flower can be 10 feet (3 m) tall. Some special gardens, which people can visit, grow this plant. Crowds line up to see the huge, smelly flower, which lives for only two or three days.

Imagine you are a plant scientist and you find a titan arum growing in a rain forest. How would you describe this flower to someone who has never seen it?

Big, Small, and Even Round

There are nearly half a million different types of plants on Earth.

Luckily, most don't smell like the titan arum.

Plants come in many different sizes, from tiny moss plants to giant sequoia (sih-KWOI-uh) trees.

Plants grow in lots of different shapes, too.

It's not hard to see how the baseball plant got its name!

snail

tiny moss plant

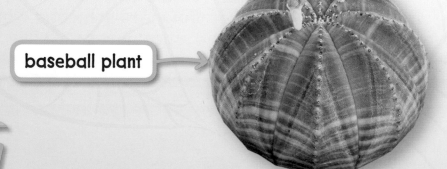

baseball plant

Giant sequoia trees are the largest trees on Earth. Their huge trunks can measure more than 100 feet (30 m) around the bottom. That's about as big as 16 tall grown-ups lying head to toe in the shape of a circle.

trunks of giant sequoia trees

A Giant Tree Trunk

Around 2,000 years ago, a little cypress tree **seed** began to grow in Mexico.

As the tree grew, its trunk got bigger and bigger.

Today, at its widest point, the tree's trunk measures more than 114 feet (35 m) across.

It is one of the biggest tree trunks on Earth!

The giant tree is known as the Tule (TOO-lee) tree.

The Tule tree grows in the town of Santa María del Tule in Mexico.

The Tule tree's trunk does not have a round shape. If a giant slice was cut out of the trunk and seen from above, it would look very curvy.

the shape of the Tule tree's trunk

the Tule tree

The Oldest Trees

The giant Tule tree is about 2,000 years old, but some trees are even older.

It's possible to see how old a tree is by looking at the wood in its trunk.

A tree grows some new wood under its **bark** every year.

If a trunk is sliced, each year's new growth will look like a ring.

Scientists have counted the rings in the trunks of some bristlecone pine trees.

They found out that the trees are nearly 5,000 years old!

United States

Atlantic Ocean

Pacific Ocean

N
W   E
S

Where bristlecone pine trees grow

slice of a tree trunk

rings

bristlecone pine tree

Scientists don't want to cut down a very old tree to count its rings. Instead, they use a special drill that cuts and pulls out a thin piece of wood from inside its trunk—without harming the tree. Then they count the rings in this piece of wood.

Giant Pinecones

Pine trees grow cones with spiky **scales**.

The tree's seeds form inside the cones.

When the seeds are fully grown, the cones' scales open up.

The seeds fall to the ground, ready to grow into new trees.

Some pine trees have giant cones.

Sugar pine tree cones can grow up to 24 inches (61 cm) long!

sugar pinecone

pinecone with closed scales

pinecone with open scales

pine tree seeds

Coulter pinecone

A Coulter pine tree cone may be 14 inches (36 cm) long and weigh 10 pounds (4.5 kg). That's as heavy as some bowling balls.

United States

Atlantic Ocean

Pacific Ocean

Mexico

N
W E
S

In North America, Coulter pine trees and sugar pine trees grow in forests in Oregon, California, and Mexico, shown in red.

Is It a Leaf or a Boat?

It's not just trees and cones that can grow to giant sizes—leaves can, too!

The giant water lily plant grows in the mud at the bottom of rivers.

The plant's leaves float on the water's surface.

The leaves can grow to more than eight feet (2.4 m) across.

They are strong enough to hold a child!

Could you and a friend lie head to toe in a giant water lily leaf? Find out by measuring an eight foot (2.4 m) piece of string. Now lie down with your friend next to the string. Will you both fit?

The bottom of a giant water lily's leaf has ribs with sharp spines. Air gets trapped between the ribs and helps the leaf float. The prickly spines protect the leaf from fish and other animals that might eat it.

rib

spine

bottom of a giant water lily leaf

giant water lily leaf

NORTH AMERICA

Atlantic Ocean

Pacific Ocean

SOUTH AMERICA

N W E S

Giant water lilies grow in rivers and ponds in the Amazon rain forest, shown in red.

15

The Smallest Flowering Plants

Not all extreme plants are giants.

Duckweed plants are the smallest flowering plants on Earth.

More than 5,000 of these tiny plants can fit inside a small soda bottle cap.

Duckweed plants are shaped like little soccer balls and have no stems, leaves, or **roots**.

The mini plants grow flowers, but they can be seen only under a **microscope**.

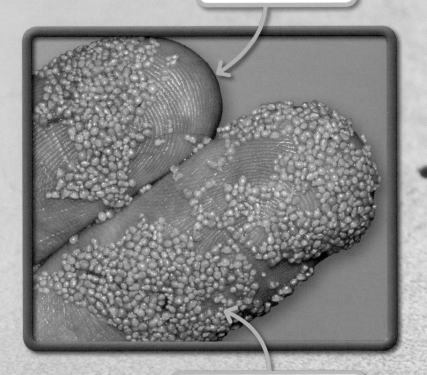

an adult's finger

Each tiny green ball is a duckweed plant.

Duckweed grows in ponds and rivers all over the world. The tiny plants float on top of the water. They spread to new places by being carried on the feet and feathers of waterbirds.

pond water covered in duckweed

A Ghostly Plant

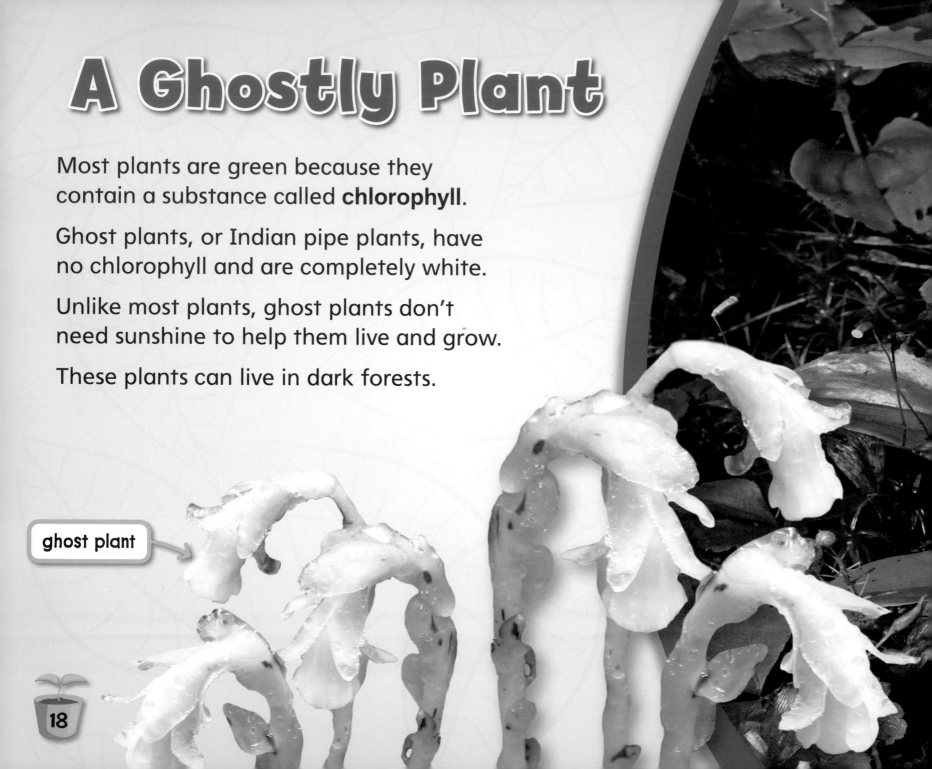

Most plants are green because they contain a substance called **chlorophyll**.

Ghost plants, or Indian pipe plants, have no chlorophyll and are completely white.

Unlike most plants, ghost plants don't need sunshine to help them live and grow.

These plants can live in dark forests.

ghost plant

Ghost plants grow to about six inches (15 cm) tall. When the plants die, or if the flowers are picked, they turn black.

The Freakiest of Them All

Tree tumbos grow in the hot, dry Namib Desert in Africa. They can live to be more than 1,000 years old. In all that time, they grow only two leaves!

A plant called the tree tumbo is perhaps the world's freakiest plant.

It's hard to believe, but this plant grows only two very long leaves.

Over many years, the leaves get torn by the wind and tangled together.

Some plants, like the tree tumbo, can be ugly.

Others can be huge, tiny, or even stinky.

One thing is for sure—the world is filled with freaky and amazing plants!

leaf

tree tumbo

AFRICA

Atlantic Ocean

Indian Ocean

N
W E
S

Where tree tumbos live

Science Lab

Plant Treasure Hunt

Amazing and freaky plants don't grow just in faraway rain forests or deserts.

Go on a plant treasure hunt to discover what's growing in your backyard or at a nearby park.

See how many of these things you can find:

- A tiny moss plant
- A leaf that is bigger than your hand or your face
- A flower or leaf that is smaller than your little fingernail
- A tree with a very thick trunk
- A tree with a crooked shape
- A tree stump with rings you can count
- A plant with a stinky smell
- A pinecone
- Something you think is amazing or unusual

Pinecone Experiment

When it rains, the scales on a pine tree cone close up to stop the seeds inside from getting wet.

You can test this for yourself.

Put a pinecone with open scales in an empty jar.

Fill the jar to the top with water and screw on the lid.

Watch what happens.

When the cone's scales have closed up, take it out of the jar.

Put the cone somewhere warm or sunny to dry.

What happens next?

Science Words

bark (BARK) the tough outer covering of a tree's trunk

chlorophyll (KLOR-uh-fil) the substance in leaves that traps sunlight and uses it to make a plant's food; it gives the plant its green color

microscope (MYE-kruh-skohp) a tool used to see things that are too small to see with the eyes alone

roots (ROOTS) underground parts of plants that take in water and nutrients from the soil; roots spread out in the soil to hold a plant in place

scales (SKAYLZ) small overlapping sections

seed (SEED) a small part of a plant that can grow into a new plant

Index

Read More

Chin, Jason. *Redwoods*. New York: Flashpoint/Roaring Book Press (2009).

Lawrence, Ellen. *Amazing Plant Bodies: Tiny to Gigantic (Plant-ology)*. New York: Bearport (2013).

Souza, D. M. *Freaky Flowers*. New York: Scholastic (2002).

Learn More Online

To learn more about freaky plants, visit
www.bearportpublishing.com/Plant-ology

About the Author

Ellen Lawrence lives in the United Kingdom. Her favorite books to write are those about nature and animals. In fact, the first book Ellen bought for herself, when she was six years old, was the story of a gorilla named Patty Cake that was born in New York's Central Park Zoo.